THIS COLORING BOOK BELONGS TO

____

Merry Christmas!

MERRY
CHRISTMAS

Merry Christmas!

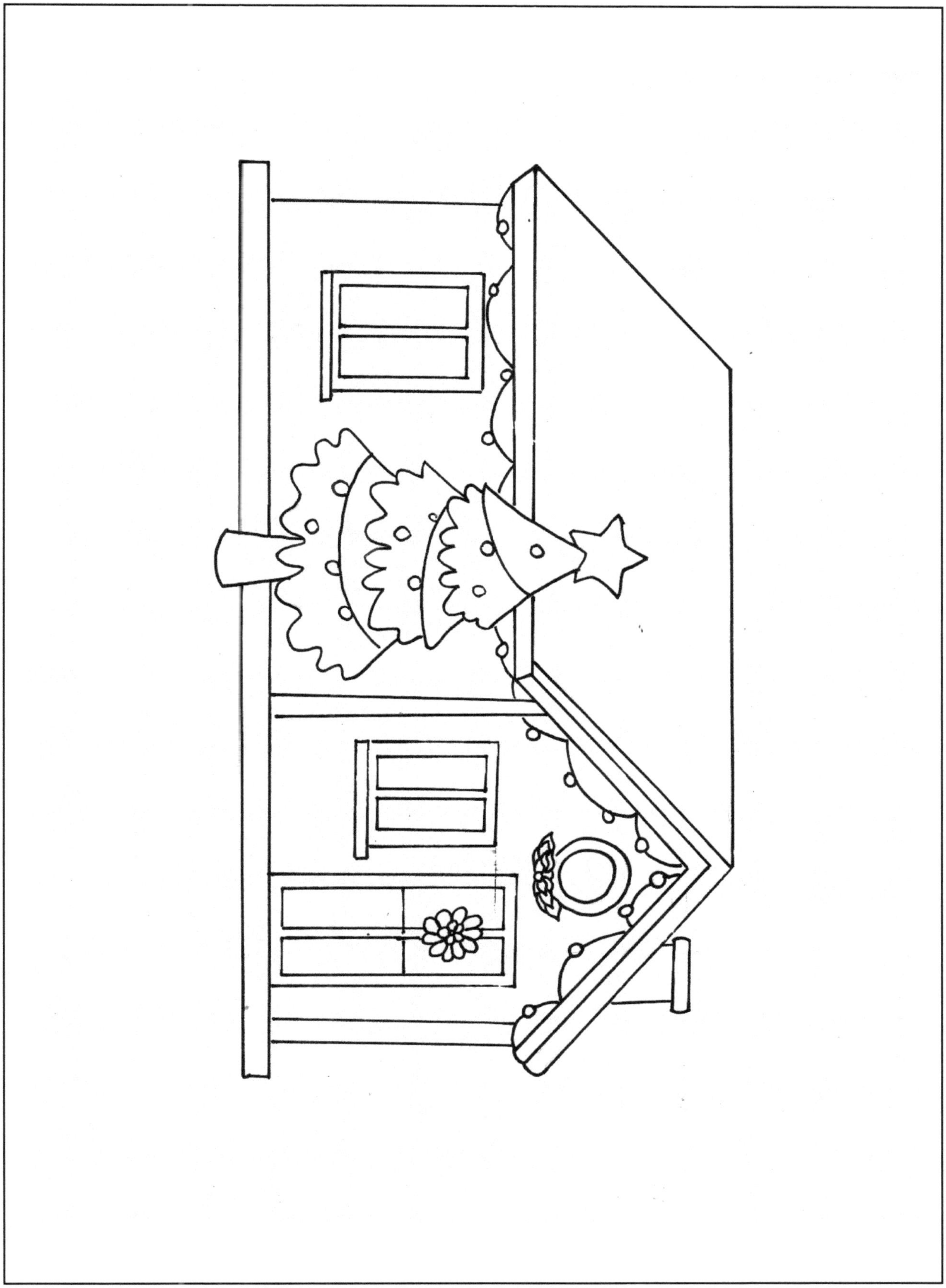

Merry Christmas!

www.ingramcontent.com/pod-product-compliance
Lightning Source LLC
LaVergne TN
LVHW070750211224
799664LV00015B/1343
9798583470341